Pebble® Plus
Bilingüe/Bilingual

Investiga las estaciones/Investigate the Seasons

Veamos el verano/ Let's Look at Summer

por/by Sarah L. Schuette

Traducción/Translation: Dr. Martín Luis Guzmán Ferrer
Editor Consultor/Consulting Editor: Dra. Gail Saunders-Smith

Capstone press®

Mankato, Minnesota

Pebble Plus is published by Capstone Press,
151 Good Counsel Drive, P.O. Box 669, Mankato, Minnesota 56002.
www.capstonepress.com

1 2 3 4 5 6 13 12 11 10 09 08

Library of Congress Cataloging-in-Publication Data
Schuette, Sarah L., 1976–
    [Let's look at summer. Spanish & English]
    Veamos el verano / por Sarah L. Schuette = Let's look at summer / by Sarah L. Schuette.
    p. cm. — (Pebble Plus. Investiga las estaciones = Investigate the seasons)
    Includes index.
    ISBN-13: 978-1-4296-2290-5 (hardcover)
    ISBN-10: 1-4296-2290-3 (hardcover)
    1. Animal behavior — Juvenile literature. 2. Summer — Juvenile literature. I. Title. II. Title: Let's look at
summer. III. Series.
QL753.S38318 2009
508.2 — dc22
        2008004832

Summary: Simple text and photographs present what happens to the weather, animals, and
    plants in summer — in both English and Spanish.

Editorial Credits
Martha E. H. Rustad, editor; Katy Kudela, bilingual editor; Adalín Torres-Zayas, Spanish copy editor;
    Bobbi J. Wyss, set designer; Veronica Bianchini, book designer; Kara Birr, photo researcher;
    Scott Thoms, photo editor

Photo Credits
Bruce Coleman Inc./Kim Taylor, 11
Corbis/Donna Disario, cover (background tree)
Getty Images Inc./Photographer's Choice/Darrell Gulin, 14–15; Photographer's Choice/Gail Shumway, 13;
    Photonica/Farhad J. Parsa, 7
Shutterstock/Andre Nantel, 20–21; bora ucak, cover, 1 (magnifying glass); Christopher, 1 (sun); Joe Gough,
cover (inset leaf); Kotelnikov Sergey, 18–19; Brian Erickson, 5
UNICORN Stock Photos/Jim Shippee, 16–17; Paula J. Harrington, 8–9

The author dedicates this book to her neighbor, Helen Reinhardt of Henderson, Minnesota.

Note to Parents and Teachers

The Investiga las estaciones/Investigate the Seasons set supports national science
standards related to weather and climate. This book describes and illustrates summer
in both English and Spanish. The images support early readers in understanding the text.
The repetition of words and phrases helps early readers learn new words. This book also
introduces early readers to subject-specific vocabulary words, which are defined in the
Glossary section. Early readers may need assistance to read some words and to use the
Table of Contents, Glossary, Internet Sites, and Index sections of the book.

Table of Contents

Tabla de contenidos

It's Summer!

How do you know it's summer?

The temperature rises.

It's the warmest season.

¡Es verano!

¿Cómo sabemos que es verano?

Sube la temperatura.

Es la estación más

calurosa del año.

The sun shines high
in the sky. Summer days
are the longest of the year.

El Sol brilla en lo alto
del cielo. Los días de verano
son los más largos del año.

Animals in Summer

What do animals do
in summer? Deer rest in
the shade to keep cool.

Los animales en verano

¿Qué hacen los animales en
verano? Los venados descansan
en la sombra para estar frescos.

Tadpoles grow into
young frogs. They find
lots of bugs to eat.

Los renacuajos se convierten
en ranas jóvenes. Encuentran
muchos insectos para comérselos.

Fireflies light up on
summer nights. They
flash to find mates.

Las luciérnagas iluminan
las noches de verano.
Relampaguean para
encontrar pareja.

Plants in Summer

What happens to plants in summer? Trees are full of green leaves.

Las plantas en verano

¿Qué les pasa a las plantas en verano? Los árboles se llenan de hojas verdes.

Plump cherries hang from branches. They are a tasty summer treat.

Cerezas regordetas cuelgan de las ramas. Son muy deliciosas y dulces en el verano.

Sunflowers turn toward the sun. They grow taller with the warm sunshine.

Los girasoles voltean hacia el Sol. Crecen muy altos con la cálida luz del sol.

What's Next?

The weather gets colder.

Summer is over.

What season comes next?

¿Qué le sigue?

El clima es cada vez más fresco.

Ha terminado el verano.

¿Cuál es la siguiente estación?

Glossary

mate — a partner or one of a pair; fireflies flash their lights to attract mates.

season — one of the four parts of the year; winter, spring, summer, and fall are seasons.

shade — an area out of the sun

tadpole — a young frog; tadpoles hatch from eggs and swim in water.

temperature — the measure of how hot or cold something is

Glosario

la estación — una de las cuatro épocas del año; el invierno, la primavera, el verano y el otoño son estaciones.

la pareja — compañero o uno de un par; las luciérnagas relampaguean sus luces para atraer una pareja.

el renacuajo — rana joven; los renacuajos nacen de huevos y nadan en el agua.

la sombra — área que está fuera del Sol

la temperatura — medida de qué tan frío o caliente está una cosa

Internet Sites

FactHound offers a safe, fun way to find Internet sites related to this book. All of the sites on FactHound have been researched by our staff.

Here's how:

1. Visit *www.facthound.com*

2. Choose your grade level.

3. Type in this book ID **1429622903** for age-appropriate sites. You may also browse subjects by clicking on letters, or by clicking on pictures and words.

4. Click on the **Fetch It** button.

FactHound will fetch the best sites for you!

Sitios de Internet

FactHound te brinda una manera divertida y segura de encontrar sitios de Internet relacionados con este libro. Hemos investigado todos los sitios de FactHound. Es posible que algunos sitios no estén en español.

Se hace así:

1. Visita *www.facthound.com*

2. Elige tu grado escolar.

3. Introduce este código especial **1429622903** para ver sitios apropiados a tu edad, o usa una palabra relacionada con este libro para hacer una búsqueda general.

4. Haz un clic en el botón **Fetch It**.

¡FactHound buscará los mejores sitios para ti!

Index

Índice